Bats Versus Bugs

by Isabel Thomas

illustrated by Maxine Lee-Mackie

OXFORD
UNIVERSITY PRESS

Bats Munch Moths

It is a dark night.
Look out for bats!

The air is thick with bats.

The bats look for bugs to munch.

Bats have big ears.
They can hear moths.

This bat gets a moth.

The bat zooms back to the cavern.

It feeds the moth to its pup.

The bats hang out in the cavern.
They are in luck!
They get lots of moths.

Bats need to look out for bugs, too!

Bugs Munch Bats

This long bug is looking for food. It likes to munch bats.

The bug hangs down and waits.

The bug has big fangs.
It swings to grab the bat.

The bat avoids the big fangs.
It zooms off.

It meets a bigger set of fangs.
Bugs need dinner, too!

Encourage students to use the pictures to explain how the bat and the bug feed.